Unlocking Property Gold

Insider Strategies for Real Estate Prosperity

NELLA BYRAN

Copyright

No part of this should be reproduced without the permission of the author.

© Nella Byran 2024

Contents

Introduction 4
The Foundation of Real Estate Wealth 7
Understanding Market Dynamics 11
Navigating Property Types 15
Financing Your Investments 20
Location: The Key to Success 25
Analyzing Risk and Reward 30
Negotiation Tactics for Profit 36
Maximizing Rental Income 41
Flipping Properties for Quick Returns 47
Harnessing the Power of Technology in Real Estate 54
Building a Strong Real Estate Network 61
Legal Considerations Every Investor Should Know 67
Sustainable Investing Practices 74
Adapting to Market Cycles 81
Exit Strategies: Knowing When to Sell 88
Scaling Your Real Estate Portfolio 95
Overcoming Common Pitfalls 102
The Future of Real Estate Investing 109

Introduction

In the ever-evolving world of real estate, fortunes are made and dreams are realized through the mastery of its intricate landscape. Welcome to "Unlocking Property Gold: Insider Strategies for Real Estate Prosperity." Within these pages lie the keys to unlocking the vast potential and hidden treasures that lie within the realm of property investment.

Real estate is more than just bricks and mortar; it's a dynamic and multifaceted industry where savvy investors thrive and opportunities abound. Whether you're a seasoned investor looking to expand your portfolio or a newcomer eager to embark on your journey to financial freedom, this book is your essential guide to navigating the labyrinth of real estate with confidence and finesse.

Drawing upon decades of collective experience and insider knowledge, we delve deep into the strategies, tactics, and principles that separate the successful from the merely aspirational in the world of real estate. From understanding market dynamics to mastering negotiation techniques, each chapter is crafted to empower you with the tools and insights needed to prosper in any economic climate.

But this book is more than just a roadmap to financial success; it's a manifesto for those who dare to dream big and aspire to create lasting wealth through the power of real estate. Whether your goal is to build a diverse portfolio of rental properties, flip houses for quick profits, or develop commercial ventures that leave a lasting impact on communities, "Unlocking Property Gold" equips you with the knowledge and strategies to turn your ambitions into reality.

As you embark on this transformative journey, remember that success in real estate is not solely measured by monetary gains but by the lives you touch, the communities you enrich, and the legacies you build. It's about embracing innovation, adapting to change, and always staying one step ahead of the curve.

So, dear reader, let us embark together on this odyssey into the heart of real estate prosperity. Let us unlock the hidden potential of properties, uncover the secrets of success, and forge our paths towards a future filled with abundance, fulfillment, and infinite possibilities. The keys to property gold await – are you ready to seize them?

The Foundation of Real Estate Wealth

The foundation of real estate wealth is rooted in several key principles that serve as the bedrock for success in the industry. Understanding and mastering these foundational elements is crucial for anyone looking to build a sustainable and profitable real estate portfolio.

First and foremost, a solid understanding of fundamental real estate concepts is essential. This includes grasping basic terminology, such as appreciation, cash flow, leverage, and cap rates, as well as understanding the various types of real estate investments, from residential to commercial, and everything in between. Without this foundational knowledge, navigating the complexities of the real estate market can be daunting and potentially risky.

Furthermore, financial literacy plays a pivotal role in building real estate wealth. This involves understanding concepts such as return on investment (ROI), net operating income (NOI), and debt-to-equity ratios. A strong grasp of financial principles allows investors to make informed decisions about which properties to acquire, when to buy or sell, and how to optimize their investment returns over time.

Another cornerstone of real estate wealth is market analysis. Successful investors know how to research and evaluate market trends, demographic data, and economic indicators to identify lucrative investment opportunities. This involves analyzing supply and demand dynamics, vacancy rates, rental yields, and other factors that influence property values and rental income. By staying informed about market conditions, investors can position themselves to capitalize on emerging trends and avoid potential pitfalls.

Risk management is also a critical component of the foundation of real estate wealth. Investing in real estate inherently involves a degree of risk, whether it be market fluctuations, property damage, or tenant issues. Successful investors mitigate these risks through careful due diligence, thorough property inspections, proper insurance coverage, and prudent financial planning. Additionally, diversification across different types of properties and geographic locations can help spread risk and protect against downturns in specific markets.

Moreover, building strong relationships and networks within the real estate industry is vital for long-term success. From real estate agents and brokers to lenders, contractors, and property managers, cultivating a reliable team of professionals can provide valuable support and expertise throughout the investment process. Networking also opens doors to new opportunities, off-market deals, and potential partnerships that can accelerate wealth-building efforts.

Ultimately, the foundation of real estate wealth is built upon knowledge, financial acumen, market savvy, risk management, and relationships. By mastering these foundational elements and applying them diligently, investors can unlock the full potential of real estate as a vehicle for building wealth and achieving financial freedom.

Understanding Market Dynamics

Understanding market dynamics is paramount for success in real estate investment. It entails comprehending the intricate interplay of supply and demand, economic factors, and consumer behavior that shape the performance of property markets. By gaining insights into market dynamics, investors can make informed decisions, identify lucrative opportunities, and mitigate risks effectively.

One fundamental aspect of market dynamics is supply and demand. Real estate markets are influenced by the balance between the availability of properties (supply) and the desire or need for those properties (demand). Understanding the current and projected levels of supply and demand within specific geographic areas and property types is essential for assessing investment potential. For instance, areas experiencing population growth or economic expansion may have increasing demand for housing, while oversaturated markets may present challenges for investors.

Economic factors also play a significant role in shaping market dynamics. Variables such as employment rates, income levels, interest rates, and GDP growth impact consumer confidence and purchasing power, thereby influencing demand for real estate. Additionally, factors like inflation, monetary policy, and global economic trends can affect property values and investment returns. Investors need to stay abreast of economic indicators and trends to anticipate market shifts and adjust their strategies accordingly.

Consumer behavior is another critical aspect of market dynamics. Understanding the preferences, needs, and motivations of potential buyers or renters can inform investment decisions and property management strategies. Factors such as demographic trends, lifestyle preferences, and cultural shifts influence the demand for specific types of properties, amenities, and location preferences. By aligning investments with market demand and consumer preferences, investors can maximize rental income, property appreciation, and overall returns.

Moreover, market dynamics vary across different property sectors and geographic regions. Residential, commercial, industrial, and retail real estate markets each have unique characteristics, drivers, and cycles. Factors such as zoning regulations, infrastructure development, and urbanization trends further contribute to market differentiation. Investors must conduct thorough market research and analysis tailored to the specific sector and location of interest to identify opportunities and risks effectively.

In today's digital age, technology also plays a crucial role in shaping market dynamics. Real estate data analytics, predictive modeling, and online platforms provide investors with access to vast amounts of information and insights. Leveraging technology tools allows investors to conduct comprehensive market research, evaluate property performance, and track trends in real-time, enhancing decision-making capabilities and competitive advantage.

In conclusion, understanding market dynamics is essential for success in real estate investment. By analyzing supply and demand dynamics, economic factors, consumer behavior, sectoral variations, and technological advancements, investors can navigate complex markets, identify opportunities, and optimize investment strategies for long-term prosperity.

Navigating Property Types

Navigating property types is a crucial aspect of real estate investment, as different property types offer unique opportunities, challenges, and investment strategies. Understanding the characteristics, demand drivers, and investment considerations associated with various property types is essential for investors to make informed decisions and build a diversified portfolio tailored to their goals and risk tolerance.

Residential Properties

Residential properties encompass a wide range of housing options, including single-family homes, condominiums, townhouses, apartments, and multi-family buildings. These properties are primarily used for residential purposes and are typically leased to tenants or occupied by homeowners. Residential real estate offers stability, steady cash flow, and a diverse tenant pool, making it an attractive option for both novice and seasoned investors. Factors such as location, neighborhood demographics, rental demand, and property condition influence the performance and profitability of residential investments.

Commercial Properties

Commercial properties are real estate assets used for business purposes, such as office buildings, retail centers, industrial warehouses, and mixed-use developments. Investing in commercial real estate offers potential for higher rental income and property appreciation but also entails greater complexity and risk compared to residential properties. Factors such as lease terms, tenant creditworthiness, market demand, and economic trends impact the performance of commercial investments. Moreover, different asset classes within commercial real estate have unique dynamics and considerations, requiring specialized knowledge and expertise.

Industrial Properties

Industrial properties encompass facilities used for manufacturing, distribution, storage, and logistics purposes, such as warehouses, distribution centers, and industrial parks. Industrial real estate has gained prominence in recent years due to the growth of e-commerce, globalization, and supply chain optimization. Investing in industrial properties offers stable cash flow, long-term leases, and potential for capital appreciation driven by increasing demand for logistics and warehousing space. Factors such as location, proximity to transportation networks, building specifications, and tenant quality influence the performance of industrial investments.

Retail Properties

Retail properties include shopping centers, malls, strip malls, standalone retail stores, and mixed-use developments with retail components. The retail sector is highly diverse, encompassing a wide range of businesses, formats, and consumer preferences. Investing in retail real estate requires careful consideration of factors such as tenant mix, foot traffic, anchor tenants, lease structures, and competition from e-commerce. Retail investments can offer steady cash flow and potential for value creation through active management and repositioning strategies.

Specialized Properties

Specialized properties encompass niche asset classes with unique characteristics and usage requirements, such as hotels, healthcare facilities, senior housing, self-storage facilities, and student housing. Investing in specialized properties offers opportunities for diversification and higher returns but also requires specialized knowledge and expertise. Factors such as regulatory requirements, demographic trends, market demand, and operational considerations influence the performance of specialized investments.

In summary, navigating property types requires investors to understand the nuances, demand drivers, and investment considerations associated with each asset class. By conducting thorough market research, assessing risk factors, and aligning investments with their objectives and risk tolerance, investors can build a diversified real estate portfolio that maximizes returns and mitigates risks over the long term.

Financing Your Investments

Financing your real estate investments is a critical aspect of success in the industry, as it determines your ability to acquire properties, manage cash flow, and maximize returns. Effective financing strategies can help investors leverage their capital, mitigate risks, and unlock new opportunities in the market. In this chapter, we'll explore various financing options available to real estate investors and discuss key considerations for choosing the right approach for your investment goals and financial situation.

Traditional Financing

One of the most common methods of financing real estate investments is through traditional mortgage loans offered by banks, credit unions, and mortgage lenders. These loans typically require a down payment ranging from 3% to 20%

of the property's purchase price, depending on factors such as creditworthiness, loan type, and property type. Traditional financing options include fixed-rate mortgages, adjustable-rate mortgages (ARMs), and government-backed loans such as FHA, VA, and USDA loans. Investors can leverage traditional financing to acquire residential and commercial properties for rental income or long-term appreciation.

Private Lending

Private lending involves borrowing money from individuals or private investment firms rather than traditional financial institutions. Private lenders may offer more flexible terms, faster approval processes, and higher loan-to-value (LTV) ratios than traditional lenders, making them an attractive option for investors seeking alternative financing solutions. Private lending arrangements may include short-term bridge loans, hard money loans, or private equity partnerships, depending on the specific needs and preferences of the investor.

Seller Financing

Seller financing, also known as owner financing or seller carryback, occurs when the property seller agrees to finance all or part of the purchase price for the buyer. In a seller financing arrangement, the buyer makes periodic payments to the seller, typically with interest, until the loan is fully repaid. Seller financing can benefit both parties by facilitating the sale of properties in a competitive market while providing the buyer with alternative financing options and potentially favorable terms. Seller financing arrangements may include installment sales contracts, land contracts, or lease-purchase agreements, depending on the terms negotiated between the buyer and seller.

Creative Financing Strategies

Real estate investors can also employ creative financing strategies to structure deals and leverage existing assets to fund new investments. Examples of creative financing techniques include seller leasebacks, subject-to financing, wraparound mortgages, and equity sharing agreements. These strategies require careful planning, negotiation, and due diligence to ensure compliance with legal and regulatory requirements while maximizing financial benefits for all parties involved.

Crowdfunding and Syndication

With the rise of technology and online platforms, crowdfunding and syndication have emerged as alternative methods of financing real estate investments. Crowdfunding platforms allow individual investors to pool their resources and invest in real estate projects collectively, while syndication involves partnering with other investors or syndicators to acquire properties through joint ventures or limited liability companies (LLCs). Crowdfunding and syndication offer opportunities for diversification, access to institutional-grade assets, and passive income streams for investors with varying levels of capital and expertise.

In conclusion, financing your real estate investments requires careful consideration of various factors, including your investment objectives, risk tolerance, creditworthiness, and available resources. By exploring different financing options, leveraging creative strategies, and seeking professional guidance when necessary, investors can effectively fund their real estate ventures and achieve their financial goals in the dynamic and competitive real estate market.

Location: The Key to Success

"Location, location, location" is not just a catchy phrase; it's the mantra of successful real estate investing. The importance of location cannot be overstated in the world of property investment, as it is often the primary factor driving demand, property values, and investment returns. In this chapter, we delve into why location is the key to success in real estate and how investors can identify and capitalize on prime locations to maximize their investment potential.

Proximity to Amenities and Services

One of the most significant factors that determine a property's desirability and value is its proximity to essential amenities and services. Properties located near schools, hospitals, shopping centers, restaurants, parks, public transportation, and other conveniences are more attractive to tenants and buyers alike. Access to amenities enhances the quality of life for residents and increases the demand for properties in these areas, driving up rental rates and property values over time.

Neighborhood Quality and Safety

The overall quality and safety of a neighborhood play a crucial role in determining its attractiveness to residents and investors. Properties located in safe, well-maintained neighborhoods with low crime rates, good schools, and strong community amenities tend to command higher rents and prices than those in less desirable areas. Investing in properties in stable, up-and-coming neighborhoods with potential for growth and revitalization can yield significant long-term returns and mitigate investment risks.

Job Market and Economic Opportunities

The strength of the local job market and economic opportunities within a region have a profound impact on real estate values and investment prospects. Cities and regions with robust job growth, diverse industries, and strong economic fundamentals tend to experience higher demand for housing and commercial properties, driving up prices and rental rates. Conversely, areas with stagnant or declining economies may struggle with high vacancy rates and depressed property values. Investors should consider the economic outlook and employment trends when evaluating potential investment locations to ensure long-term viability and growth potential.

Supply and Demand Dynamics

Understanding supply and demand dynamics within a specific market is essential for identifying prime investment locations. Markets with limited inventory, high demand, and population growth are typically more favorable for investors, as they offer opportunities for appreciation and rental income growth. Conversely, oversaturated markets with excess supply may experience downward pressure on prices and rents, making it challenging to achieve favorable investment returns. Analyzing market fundamentals, such as vacancy rates, absorption rates, and population trends, can help investors identify underserved markets and capitalize on emerging opportunities.

Regulatory and Zoning Considerations

Regulatory and zoning factors can significantly impact the attractiveness and feasibility of real estate investments in certain locations. Local zoning ordinances, land use regulations, building codes, and permitting processes can affect property development, use, and investment returns. Investors should be aware of any regulatory constraints or potential changes that may affect their ability to maximize the value of their properties. Additionally, understanding tax policies, incentives, and development plans can provide insights into future growth prospects and investment opportunities within a given location.

In conclusion, location is indeed the key to success in real estate investing. By focusing on prime locations with proximity to amenities, desirable neighborhoods, strong economic fundamentals, favorable supply and demand dynamics, and conducive regulatory environments, investors can position themselves for long-term success and maximize their investment returns. Conducting thorough market research, leveraging local expertise, and staying informed about market trends and developments are essential strategies for identifying and capitalizing on lucrative investment locations in the dynamic and competitive world of real estate.

Analyzing Risk and Reward

Analyzing risk and reward is a fundamental aspect of real estate investment, as it allows investors to assess the potential benefits and pitfalls of a particular investment opportunity. By carefully evaluating the risks associated with an investment relative to the potential rewards, investors can make informed decisions, mitigate potential losses, and maximize their returns. Here's a detailed explanation of how to analyze risk and reward in real estate investment:

Identify and Assess Risks

The first step in analyzing risk and reward is to identify and assess the various risks associated with a particular investment opportunity. Risks in real estate can stem from factors such as market volatility, economic downturns, tenant turnover, property damage, regulatory changes, and financing challenges. Investors should conduct a comprehensive risk assessment by analyzing both internal and external factors that may impact the investment's performance. This includes evaluating property-specific risks, such as location, condition, and market demand, as well as broader market and economic risks that may affect the investment's viability and potential returns.

Quantify Risks

Once risks have been identified, investors should quantify the potential impact of each risk on the investment's financial performance. This involves assessing the likelihood of each risk occurring and estimating the magnitude of its potential consequences in terms of financial losses or diminished returns. Investors can use quantitative analysis techniques, such as sensitivity analysis, scenario planning, and probabilistic modeling, to assess the range of possible outcomes under different risk scenarios. By quantifying risks, investors can gain a clearer understanding of the potential downside exposure and develop risk mitigation strategies accordingly.

Evaluate Potential Rewards

In addition to assessing risks, investors must also evaluate the potential rewards associated with the investment opportunity. This involves analyzing the investment's income potential, capital appreciation prospects, tax benefits, and overall return on investment (ROI). Investors should consider factors such as rental income, occupancy rates, property appreciation rates, and potential value-add opportunities that may enhance the investment's profitability over time. By conducting a thorough analysis of potential rewards, investors can gauge the investment's upside potential and assess whether the potential returns justify the associated risks.

Calculate Risk-Adjusted Returns

Once risks and rewards have been evaluated, investors can calculate risk-adjusted returns to determine whether the investment offers an acceptable balance between risk and reward. Risk-adjusted returns take into account the level of risk associated with the investment and adjust the expected returns accordingly. Common risk-adjusted return metrics include the Sharpe ratio, the Treynor ratio, and the risk-adjusted return on investment (RAROI). These metrics help investors compare investment opportunities with varying levels of risk and assess which investments offer the best risk-adjusted return potential.

Develop Risk Mitigation Strategies

Finally, investors should develop risk mitigation strategies to minimize potential losses and protect their investment capital. Risk mitigation strategies may include diversifying the investment portfolio, implementing risk management protocols, securing appropriate insurance coverage, maintaining adequate cash reserves, and conducting thorough due diligence on potential investment opportunities. Additionally, investors can hedge against specific risks by structuring investments with favorable terms, negotiating lease agreements, and incorporating risk-sharing mechanisms into partnership agreements. By proactively addressing potential risks and implementing risk mitigation strategies, investors can safeguard their investment capital and enhance their chances of achieving favorable returns over the long term.

In conclusion, analyzing risk and reward is a critical process in real estate investment that involves identifying, quantifying, and evaluating the risks and potential rewards associated with a particular investment opportunity. By conducting thorough risk assessments, evaluating potential rewards, calculating risk-adjusted returns, and developing risk mitigation strategies, investors can make informed decisions, minimize potential losses, and maximize their chances of achieving their investment objectives in the dynamic and competitive real estate market.

Negotiation Tactics for Profit

Negotiation tactics are paramount in real estate transactions, as they can significantly impact the profitability and success of an investment. Mastering effective negotiation techniques allows investors to secure favorable terms, maximize value, and achieve their financial objectives. In this chapter, we explore key negotiation tactics that can help real estate investors negotiate for profit:

Do Your Homework

Preparation is key to successful negotiations in real estate. Before entering into negotiations, conduct thorough research on the property, market conditions, comparable sales, and the seller's motivations. Understanding the property's history, current market value, and potential for appreciation or improvement arms you with valuable information to negotiate from a position of strength.

Establish Your Objectives

Clearly define your objectives and priorities before entering negotiations. Determine your maximum purchase price, desired terms, and any non-negotiable factors. Having a clear understanding of your goals allows you to focus your negotiation efforts on achieving the best possible outcome while staying within your investment parameters.

Build Rapport and Trust

Building rapport and trust with the seller can enhance your negotiation position and increase the likelihood of a successful outcome. Take the time to establish a positive relationship with the seller, listen to their concerns, and demonstrate empathy and understanding. Building trust creates a collaborative atmosphere and increases the likelihood of reaching mutually beneficial agreements.

Focus on Value, Not Price

Instead of solely focusing on price, emphasize the value you bring to the transaction. Highlight your ability to close quickly, provide certainty of funds, or offer flexibility in terms. By demonstrating the value, you bring as a buyer, you may be able to negotiate more favorable terms or concessions from the seller without necessarily lowering the purchase price.

Use Leverage Wisely

Identify and leverage any factors that can strengthen your negotiation position. This may include factors such as multiple offers, property flaws or deficiencies, market conditions, or the seller's urgency to sell. Use these leverage points strategically to negotiate for concessions, price reductions, or favorable terms that align with your objectives.

Employ Effective Communication

Effective communication is essential in negotiations. Clearly articulate your position, interests, and rationale behind your proposals. Listen actively to the seller's concerns and address them thoughtfully. Use open-ended questions to gather information and uncover the seller's underlying motivations, needs, and pain points. Effective communication builds trust and rapport, fostering a collaborative negotiation process.

Be Willing to Walk Away

One of the most powerful negotiation tactics is the willingness to walk away from a deal if it does not meet your objectives or if the terms are unfavorable. Demonstrating a willingness to walk away communicates to the seller that you are serious and have alternatives, which can incentivize them to make concessions or improve their offer to keep the deal alive.

Negotiate Win-Win Solutions

Strive to negotiate win-win solutions that satisfy both parties' interests and objectives. Look for creative solutions or compromises that address the seller's concerns while also meeting your own needs. Collaborative negotiation fosters goodwill and long-term relationships, which can lead to future opportunities and referrals.

In conclusion, effective negotiation tactics are essential for real estate investors seeking to maximize profit and achieve favorable outcomes in transactions. By preparing thoroughly, establishing clear objectives, building rapport and trust, focusing on value, leveraging strengths, communicating effectively, being willing to walk away if necessary, and negotiating win-win solutions, investors can position themselves for success and capitalize on profitable investment opportunities in the dynamic and competitive real estate market.

Maximizing Rental Income

Maximizing rental income is a primary objective for real estate investors, as it directly impacts the profitability and long-term success of rental properties. By employing effective strategies to optimize rental income, investors can maximize cash flow, enhance property value, and achieve their financial objectives. In this chapter, we explore key tactics for maximizing rental income:

Market Research and Analysis

Conduct thorough market research and analysis to determine the optimal rental rates for your property. Research comparable rental listings in the area to understand market trends, demand dynamics, and competitive pricing. Consider factors such as location, property size, amenities, condition, and tenant preferences when setting rental rates. Pricing your rental competitively ensures maximum occupancy and rental income potential.

Property Upgrades and Renovations

Invest in property upgrades and renovations to enhance its appeal and justify higher rental rates. Focus on cosmetic improvements, such as fresh paint, modern fixtures, upgraded appliances, and landscaping enhancements, that add value and attract quality tenants. Consider incorporating energy-efficient features or smart home technology to appeal to modern renters and command premium rents. Well-maintained, updated properties are more likely to attract tenants willing to pay higher rents, thereby maximizing rental income.

Offer Additional Amenities and Services

Consider offering additional amenities and services to differentiate your property and justify higher rents. This may include amenities such as onsite laundry facilities, parking spaces, storage units, fitness centers, community spaces, or concierge services. Providing value-added amenities enhances the tenant experience and increases the perceived value of the rental property, allowing you to command premium rents and maximize rental income.

Implement Strategic Rent Increases

Regularly review and adjust rental rates to keep pace with market trends and inflation. Implement strategic rent increases at lease renewal or lease expiration to reflect improvements in the property, changes in market conditions, or inflationary pressures. Communicate rent increases transparently and proactively to tenants, providing justification for the adjustments and emphasizing the value they receive from the property. Incremental rent increases over time allow you to maximize rental income while maintaining tenant satisfaction and retention.

Minimize Vacancy and Turnover

Minimize vacancy and turnover to maximize rental income and cash flow. Implement proactive tenant retention strategies, such as offering lease incentives, providing exceptional customer service, addressing maintenance issues promptly, and fostering positive tenant relationships. Conduct regular property inspections and preventive maintenance to ensure tenant satisfaction and mitigate turnover risks. Minimizing vacancy and turnover reduces income loss and leasing expenses, allowing you to maximize rental income and profitability over the long term.

Screen Tenants Effectively

Screen tenants effectively to minimize the risk of rent defaults, property damage, and evictions. Implement comprehensive tenant screening criteria, including credit checks, income verification, rental history, and criminal background checks, to identify qualified and reliable tenants. Selecting high-quality tenants who pay rent on time and respect the property minimizes income disruptions and rental income losses, allowing you to maximize rental income and investment returns.

Explore Additional Revenue Streams

Explore additional revenue streams beyond traditional rent payments to maximize rental income. This may include offering pet fees, parking fees, storage rental, laundry fees, application fees, or late payment penalties to generate supplemental income from your rental property. However, be mindful of local regulations and fair housing laws when implementing additional fees and charges to ensure compliance and avoid legal issues.

In conclusion, maximizing rental income requires a strategic approach focused on market analysis, property upgrades, value-added amenities, rent optimization, tenant retention, and revenue diversification. By employing effective strategies to attract quality tenants, maintain high occupancy rates, and optimize rental rates, investors can maximize cash flow, enhance property value, and achieve long-term success in the competitive rental market.

Flipping Properties for Quick Returns

Flipping properties for quick returns involves purchasing distressed or undervalued properties, renovating or improving them, and selling them for a profit within a relatively short timeframe. This strategy requires careful planning, efficient execution, and market savvy to maximize returns and minimize risks. In this chapter, we explore key tactics for successfully flipping properties for quick returns:

Identify Profitable Opportunities

Conduct thorough market research to identify profitable flipping opportunities in areas with high demand, favorable market conditions, and potential for property appreciation. Look for distressed properties, foreclosures, short sales, or motivated sellers who are willing to sell below market value. Analyze comparable sales, market trends, and property values to assess the profit potential of each opportunity and determine whether it aligns with your investment goals.

Run the Numbers

Perform a detailed financial analysis to determine the feasibility and profitability of the flipping project. Calculate all acquisition costs, renovation expenses, carrying costs, and selling expenses to estimate the total investment required. Factor in a contingency reserve for unexpected costs or delays. Compare the projected costs against the expected sale price to determine the potential profit margin and return on investment (ROI). Ensure that the potential profit justifies the risks and effort involved in the flipping project.

Secure Financing

Secure financing for the flipping project to fund the acquisition and renovation costs. Explore financing options such as traditional mortgages, hard money loans, private lenders, or cash reserves. Choose the financing option that best aligns with your financial situation, investment objectives, and timeline. Obtain pre-approval or funding commitments before making offers on properties to demonstrate your credibility and ability to close quickly.

Negotiate Favorable Terms

Negotiate favorable terms with sellers to maximize your profit potential and minimize acquisition costs. Look for motivated sellers who are willing to negotiate on price, terms, or closing timeline. Consider including contingency clauses, inspection contingencies, or seller concessions to protect your interests and mitigate risks. Negotiate for a purchase price below market value to create a buffer for renovation expenses and potential unforeseen costs.

Renovate Strategically

Renovate the property strategically to maximize its appeal, value, and marketability while staying within budget and timeline constraints. Focus on cost-effective improvements that yield the highest return on investment, such as kitchen and bathroom upgrades, cosmetic enhancements, curb appeal enhancements, and energy-efficient features. Prioritize repairs and upgrades that address critical issues, enhance the property's aesthetics, and align with buyer preferences in the local market. Obtain multiple bids from contractors and subcontractors to ensure competitive pricing and quality workmanship.

Stage and Market Effectively

Stage the property effectively to showcase its potential and appeal to potential buyers. Invest in professional staging services or stage the property yourself using stylish furniture, décor, and accessories that highlight its features and functionality. Develop a comprehensive marketing plan to reach potential buyers through multiple channels, such as online listings, social media, print advertising, signage, and open houses. Highlight the property's unique selling points, renovations, and upgrades to attract buyer interest and generate competitive offers.

Price Competitively

Price the property competitively to generate interest and offers from motivated buyers. Consult with a real estate agent or appraiser to determine the optimal listing price based on comparable sales, market trends, and property condition. Set the price strategically to attract attention and create a sense of urgency among potential buyers while maximizing the property's value and profit potential. Be prepared to adjust the price based on feedback from the market and buyer activity to ensure a timely sale and maximize returns.

Negotiate Offers Wisely

Negotiate offers wisely to secure the best possible sale price and terms for the property. Evaluate each offer carefully, considering factors such as offer price, financing terms, contingencies, and closing timeline. Counteroffer strategically to encourage higher bids while addressing buyer concerns or conditions. Negotiate for favorable terms, such as a quick closing, earnest money deposit, or seller concessions, to enhance your profit margin and minimize closing risks. Aim to achieve a mutually beneficial agreement that maximizes your returns and satisfies the buyer's needs.

Close the Deal Efficiently

Close the deal efficiently to realize your profits and complete the flipping project successfully. Work closely with your real estate agent, attorney, title company, and lender to ensure a smooth and timely closing process. Coordinate inspections, appraisals, and necessary paperwork to meet closing deadlines and minimize delays. Review all closing documents carefully and resolve any issues or discrepancies promptly. Once the sale is finalized, celebrate your success and prepare for your next flipping project.

In conclusion, flipping properties for quick returns requires careful planning, diligent execution, and market expertise to maximize profitability and minimize risks. By identifying profitable opportunities, running the numbers, securing financing, negotiating favorable terms, renovating strategically, staging and marketing effectively, pricing competitively, negotiating offers wisely, and closing the deal efficiently, investors can successfully flip properties for quick returns and achieve their investment objectives in the dynamic and competitive real estate market.

Harnessing the Power of Technology in Real Estate

Harnessing the power of technology in real estate has become increasingly essential in today's digital age, revolutionizing how properties are bought, sold, managed, and marketed. By leveraging technology tools and platforms, real estate professionals can streamline processes, enhance efficiency, and provide better service to clients. In this chapter, we explore how technology is transforming the real estate industry and how investors can harness its power for success:

Data Analytics and Market Insights

Technology enables access to vast amounts of data and sophisticated analytics tools that provide valuable market insights and trends. Real estate professionals can leverage data analytics to analyze market trends, track property values, forecast demand, and identify investment opportunities. By harnessing the power of data-driven insights, investors can make informed decisions, mitigate risks, and capitalize on emerging market trends to maximize returns.

Online Listing Platforms

Online listing platforms and property marketplaces have revolutionized the way properties are marketed and discovered by buyers and tenants. Platforms such as Zillow, Realtor.com, and Trulia provide comprehensive listings, high-quality photos, virtual tours, and detailed property information accessible to buyers and tenants worldwide. Real estate professionals can use online listing platforms to showcase properties, attract potential buyers, and generate leads more efficiently than traditional marketing methods.

Virtual Reality (VR) and Augmented Reality (AR)

Virtual reality (VR) and augmented reality (AR) technologies are transforming the real estate industry by offering immersive and interactive experiences for buyers and tenants. VR and AR tools allow users to explore properties virtually, visualize floor plans, and experience virtual tours from the comfort of their homes. Real estate professionals can use VR and AR technologies to showcase properties, engage clients remotely, and provide personalized experiences that enhance the property discovery and decision-making process.

Property Management Software

Property management software platforms streamline property operations, automate tasks, and optimize workflows for landlords, property managers, and investors. These software solutions offer features such as online rent collection, lease management, maintenance tracking, tenant screening, and financial reporting. By centralizing property management tasks and data in one platform, investors can improve efficiency, reduce administrative burdens, and enhance the tenant experience.

Blockchain Technology

Blockchain technology is revolutionizing the real estate industry by providing secure, transparent, and tamper-proof transaction records and smart contracts. Blockchain platforms enable secure digital transactions, title transfers, and property ownership verification without the need for intermediaries. Real estate professionals can use blockchain technology to streamline transactions, reduce fraud, eliminate paperwork, and expedite the closing process, resulting in cost savings and increased efficiency for buyers, sellers, and investors.

Artificial Intelligence (AI) and Machine Learning

Artificial intelligence (AI) and machine learning technologies are empowering real estate professionals to analyze data, automate processes, and make predictive insights. AI-powered tools can analyze market trends, predict property values, recommend investment opportunities, and personalize property recommendations for clients. Real estate investors can use AI and machine learning algorithms to identify investment opportunities, optimize property portfolios, and make data-driven decisions that maximize returns and mitigate risks.

Digital Marketing and Social Media

Digital marketing and social media platforms have become indispensable tools for real estate professionals to reach and engage with clients effectively. Real estate agents and investors can use social media platforms such as Facebook,

Instagram, and LinkedIn to showcase properties, share market insights, and engage with potential buyers, tenants, and investors. Digital marketing campaigns can target specific demographics, retarget leads, and generate qualified leads more efficiently than traditional marketing methods.

Smart Home Technology

Smart home technology is revolutionizing property management and tenant experiences by offering automation, convenience, and energy efficiency. Smart home devices such as smart thermostats, security cameras, door locks, and lighting systems enable remote monitoring, control, and management of properties. Real estate investors can integrate smart home technology into their properties to attract tenants, increase property values, and differentiate their offerings in the market.

In conclusion, harnessing the power of technology in real estate offers immense opportunities for investors to streamline processes, enhance efficiency, and maximize returns. By leveraging data analytics, online listing platforms, virtual reality, property management software, blockchain technology, artificial intelligence, digital marketing, social media, and smart home technology, investors can stay ahead of the curve, capitalize on emerging trends, and achieve success in the dynamic and competitive real estate market.

Building a Strong Real Estate Network

Building a strong real estate network is essential for success in the industry, as it provides access to valuable resources, opportunities, and support from peers and professionals. A robust network can help investors source deals, access financing, find reliable contractors, and navigate the complexities of the real estate market more effectively. In this chapter, we explore strategies for building and nurturing a strong real estate network:

Define Your Objectives

Start by defining your objectives and identifying the types of connections and resources you need to achieve your real estate goals. Determine whether you're looking to build relationships with fellow investors, real estate agents, lenders, contractors, property managers, attorneys, or other industry professionals. Clarifying your objectives will guide your networking efforts and help you focus on building relationships that align with your needs and priorities.

Attend Networking Events

Attend local real estate networking events, meetups, conferences, and industry gatherings to connect with other professionals and investors in your area. Networking events provide opportunities to exchange ideas, share experiences, and build relationships with like-minded individuals who share your passion for real estate. Be proactive in introducing yourself, asking questions, and expressing genuine interest in others' experiences and expertise.

Join Real Estate Groups and Associations

Join real estate groups, associations, clubs, and forums both online and offline to expand your network and access valuable resources and support. Look for local real estate investment clubs, landlord associations, or industry-specific groups that cater to your interests and niche. Participate actively in group discussions, share insights, and offer assistance to fellow members to build rapport and establish credibility within the community.

Utilize Social Media

Leverage social media platforms such as LinkedIn, Facebook, Twitter, and Instagram to connect with real estate professionals, investors, and industry influencers. Follow industry leaders, join real estate-related groups and communities, and engage with content by commenting, sharing, and networking online. Use social media to showcase your expertise, share valuable insights, and initiate conversations with potential collaborators and partners.

Build Relationships with Local Professionals

Cultivate relationships with local real estate agents, lenders, attorneys, contractors, property managers, and other professionals who play a crucial role in the real estate ecosystem. Establishing a network of trusted professionals allows you to access reliable referrals, resources, and expertise when needed. Take the time to meet with local professionals, learn about their services, and explore opportunities for collaboration and mutual support.

Provide Value and Be Genuine

Focus on building genuine, mutually beneficial relationships with others in the real estate industry by providing value and demonstrating authenticity. Offer assistance, share insights, and provide support to others without expecting immediate returns. Be genuine in your interactions, listen actively, and show genuine interest in others' success and well-being. Building trust and credibility takes time, but it's essential for establishing lasting connections and fostering a strong network.

Follow Up and Stay Connected

Follow up with new contacts after networking events or meetings to maintain communication and nurture relationships over time. Send personalized follow-up emails, connect on social media, or schedule follow-up calls or meetings to continue the conversation. Stay connected with your network regularly by sharing updates, sending newsletters, or organizing social gatherings or networking events. Consistent communication helps you stay top of mind and reinforces your relationships with others in your network.

Be Proactive and Persistent

Building a strong real estate network requires proactive effort and persistence. Be proactive in seeking out networking opportunities, reaching out to potential connections, and following up on leads or referrals. Stay persistent in your networking efforts, even in the face of rejection or setbacks. Building a strong network takes time and effort, but the relationships you cultivate can pay dividends in the form of valuable connections, opportunities, and support throughout your real estate journey.

In conclusion, building a strong real estate network is a valuable asset for investors seeking success in the industry. By defining your objectives, attending networking events, joining real estate groups, utilizing social media, building relationships with local professionals, providing value, staying connected, and being proactive and persistent, you can cultivate a robust network of connections that support your growth, expansion, and success in the dynamic and competitive real estate market.

Legal Considerations Every Investor Should Know

Understanding legal considerations is crucial for every real estate investor to navigate the complexities of property transactions, protect their interests, and ensure compliance with applicable laws and regulations. Ignoring legal considerations can lead to costly mistakes, disputes, or even legal liabilities. In this chapter, we explore key legal considerations that every investor should know:

Property Laws and Regulations

Familiarize yourself with relevant property laws, regulations, and zoning ordinances that govern real estate transactions in your target market. Property laws vary by jurisdiction and may dictate land use restrictions, property rights, building codes, permitting requirements, and environmental regulations. Understanding these laws helps investors assess the feasibility of property investments, identify potential risks, and ensure compliance with legal requirements.

Contract Law

Contracts are the foundation of real estate transactions and govern the rights and obligations of parties involved. Familiarize yourself with contract law principles, including offer and acceptance, consideration, capacity, legality, and enforceability. Ensure that contracts are clear, concise, and drafted in accordance with applicable legal requirements to avoid misunderstandings, disputes, or contract breaches. Consider consulting with a real estate attorney to review contracts and ensure they adequately protect your interests.

Property Ownership and Title Issues

Conduct thorough due diligence to verify property ownership and address any title issues that may affect the investment. Perform title searches, obtain title insurance, and review property records to confirm ownership, identify liens, encumbrances, easements, or restrictions that may impact the property's marketability or use. Addressing title issues upfront helps investors mitigate risks and avoid potential legal disputes or challenges during the transaction process.

Landlord-Tenant Laws

If you're investing in rental properties, familiarize yourself with landlord-tenant laws and regulations that govern landlord-tenant relationships, lease agreements, eviction procedures, rent control, security deposits, and fair housing practices. Landlord-tenant laws vary by state and locality and may impose specific rights and responsibilities on landlords and tenants. Ensure that lease agreements comply with applicable laws and include essential terms and provisions to protect your rights and mitigate risks.

Taxation and Financial Considerations

Understand the tax implications and financial considerations associated with real estate investments, including property taxes, capital gains taxes, depreciation, deductions, and financing options. Consult with tax professionals or financial advisors to develop tax-efficient investment strategies, optimize tax benefits, and minimize tax liabilities. Consider structuring investments through entities such as limited liability companies (LLCs) or partnerships to protect assets and optimize tax planning strategies.

Liability and Asset Protection

Real estate investors face various risks and liabilities, including property damage, personal injury claims, and contractual disputes. Implement asset protection strategies to shield personal assets from potential liabilities associated with real estate investments. Consider forming legal entities such as LLCs or limited partnerships to hold real estate assets, limit personal liability, and provide legal protection for investors' assets. Obtain adequate insurance coverage, such as property insurance, liability insurance, and umbrella policies, to mitigate risks and protect against unforeseen events.

Due Diligence and Risk Management

Conduct thorough due diligence to assess the risks and potential liabilities associated with real estate investments. Evaluate property condition, market trends, financial performance, tenant profiles, and regulatory compliance to identify potential risks and make informed investment decisions. Perform property inspections, review financial records, and analyze market data to mitigate risks and ensure investment viability. Consider consulting with legal professionals, real estate advisors, or property management experts to assist with due diligence and risk management efforts.

Dispute Resolution and Legal Remedies

Despite careful planning and diligence, disputes or legal issues may arise during the course of real estate transactions or property ownership. Familiarize yourself with dispute resolution mechanisms, legal remedies, and recourse options available to address conflicts or breaches of contract. Consider including dispute resolution clauses, arbitration provisions, or mediation agreements in contracts to resolve disputes efficiently and cost-effectively. Consult with legal professionals to explore legal remedies and pursue appropriate courses of action to protect your interests and rights.

In conclusion, understanding legal considerations is essential for every real estate investor to navigate the complexities of property transactions, protect their interests, and ensure compliance with applicable laws and regulations. By familiarizing themselves with property laws, contract law, title issues, landlord-tenant laws, taxation, liability protection, due diligence, dispute resolution, and legal remedies, investors can mitigate risks, avoid legal pitfalls, and achieve success in the dynamic and competitive real estate market.

Sustainable Investing Practices

Sustainable investing practices, also known as socially responsible investing (SRI) or environmental, social, and governance (ESG) investing, have gained significant traction in the real estate industry as investors increasingly prioritize environmental sustainability, social responsibility, and corporate governance in their investment decisions. Sustainable investing aims to generate positive financial returns while also creating long-term value for society and the environment. In this chapter, we explore key sustainable investing practices for real estate investors:

Environmental Sustainability

Prioritize investments in properties that demonstrate environmental sustainability and energy efficiency. Consider factors such as green building certifications (e.g., LEED certification), energy-efficient design features, renewable energy sources, water conservation measures, and sustainable materials. Investing in sustainable properties not only reduces environmental impact but also enhances property value, reduces operating costs, and attracts environmentally conscious tenants.

Social Responsibility

Incorporate social responsibility considerations into investment decisions by prioritizing properties that promote social equity, inclusivity, and community well-being. Evaluate factors such as access to affordable housing, transit options, healthcare facilities, educational institutions, and recreational amenities. Invest in properties located in diverse, vibrant communities that support social cohesion, economic development, and quality of life for residents.

Tenant Health and Wellness

Prioritize investments in properties that prioritize tenant health and wellness by providing safe, healthy, and livable environments. Consider factors such as indoor air quality, natural lighting, ventilation, acoustic comfort, and access to green spaces. Implement wellness-oriented design features and amenities, such as fitness centers, outdoor recreation areas, and biophilic design elements, to enhance tenant well-being and productivity.

Resilience and Adaptation

Assess the resilience and adaptation of properties to climate change risks, natural disasters, and other environmental hazards. Invest in properties located in regions with low susceptibility to climate-related risks, such as flooding, hurricanes, wildfires, and sea-level rise. Incorporate resilient design features, such as flood barriers, stormwater management systems, and disaster-resistant construction materials, to mitigate risks and enhance property resilience over the long term.

Community Engagement and Stakeholder Collaboration

Engage with local communities, stakeholders, and tenants to understand their needs, preferences, and concerns regarding sustainable development. Foster collaboration with community organizations, government agencies, nonprofits, and industry partners to address shared sustainability goals, promote social impact initiatives, and drive positive change. Involve tenants in sustainability efforts through education, outreach, and participation in green programs and initiatives.

Data Transparency and Reporting

Embrace transparency and accountability by disclosing ESG performance metrics, sustainability initiatives, and impact outcomes to investors, stakeholders, and the public. Implement robust data collection, measurement, and reporting mechanisms to track environmental, social, and governance indicators, such as energy consumption, carbon emissions, diversity and inclusion metrics, tenant satisfaction, and community engagement efforts. Provide transparent ESG reporting to demonstrate progress, compliance, and alignment with sustainable investing objectives.

Long-Term Value Creation

Adopt a long-term perspective in real estate investing that prioritizes sustainable value creation over short-term gains. Consider the holistic impacts of investments on financial returns, environmental stewardship, social equity, and corporate governance. Integrate sustainability considerations into investment decision-making processes, asset management strategies, and portfolio management practices to maximize long-term value and mitigate risks associated with climate change, resource scarcity, and social instability.

Continuous Improvement and Innovation

Embrace a culture of continuous improvement and innovation in sustainable investing practices by staying informed about emerging trends, technologies, and best practices. Collaborate with industry peers, research institutions, and sustainability experts to exchange knowledge, share experiences, and explore innovative solutions for addressing sustainability challenges in real estate. Embrace innovation in sustainable design, construction methods, building technologies, and operational practices to drive positive change and lead the transition toward a more sustainable built environment.

In conclusion, sustainable investing practices offer real estate investors an opportunity to generate positive financial returns while also creating value for society and the environment. By prioritizing environmental sustainability, social responsibility, tenant health and wellness, resilience and adaptation, community engagement, data transparency, long-term value creation, and continuous improvement, investors can contribute to building a more sustainable and resilient real estate market that benefits present and future generations.

Adapting to Market Cycles

Adapting to market cycles is essential for real estate investors to navigate the dynamic and cyclical nature of the real estate market effectively. Market cycles, characterized by periods of expansion, peak, contraction, and trough, influence property values, demand dynamics, financing conditions, and investment opportunities. Successful investors understand how to adapt their strategies and tactics to capitalize on market upswings, mitigate risks during downturns, and position themselves for long-term success. In this chapter, we explore key strategies for adapting to market cycles in real estate investing:

Understand Market Dynamics

Gain a deep understanding of market cycles, trends, and drivers that influence real estate market dynamics in your target locations. Monitor key indicators such as employment growth, population trends, housing supply and demand, interest rates, inflation, and economic indicators to identify market cycles and anticipate shifts in market conditions. Analyze historical data and market forecasts to assess the current phase of the market cycle and make informed investment decisions accordingly.

Diversify Your Portfolio

Diversify your real estate portfolio across different asset classes, geographic locations, and market segments to mitigate risks and capitalize on diverse investment opportunities. Invest in a mix of residential, commercial, industrial, and mixed-use properties to spread risk exposure and hedge against market volatility. Diversification allows investors to balance the potential returns and risks associated with different property types and market segments, reducing reliance on any single investment or market cycle.

Adopt a Flexible Investment Strategy

Adopt a flexible investment strategy that allows you to adapt to changing market conditions and capitalize on emerging opportunities. In a seller's market characterized by high demand and low inventory, focus on acquisition strategies such as value-add opportunities, distressed properties, or off-market deals. In a buyer's market with increased inventory and declining prices, prioritize investment strategies such as buy-and-hold, long-term leasing, or opportunistic acquisitions. Remain agile and open to adjusting your investment strategy based on evolving market dynamics and investment objectives.

Manage Cash Flow and Liquidity

Maintain adequate cash reserves and liquidity to weather market downturns, capitalize on investment opportunities, and cover unforeseen expenses or contingencies. Build a financial cushion to withstand periods of reduced cash flow, vacancy, or market uncertainty without being forced to sell properties at distressed prices. Ensure access to financing options, lines of credit, or alternative sources of capital to capitalize on market opportunities and address short-term liquidity needs during market cycles.

Focus on Value-Driven Investments

Focus on value-driven investments that offer intrinsic value and long-term growth potential, regardless of market cycles. Look for properties with strong fundamentals, positive cash flow, and potential for appreciation based on factors such as location, demand drivers, property condition, and market trends. Invest in assets with sustainable income streams, high occupancy rates, and resilient cash flow profiles that can withstand market fluctuations and deliver consistent returns over time.

Monitor and Adjust Portfolio Allocation

Continuously monitor market conditions and adjust your portfolio allocation to align with prevailing market trends and investment opportunities. Rebalance your portfolio periodically to optimize risk-adjusted returns, capitalize on undervalued assets, and reduce exposure to overvalued or high-risk investments. Shift allocation between asset classes, geographic regions, and property types based on changing market dynamics, investor preferences, and risk-return profiles to optimize portfolio performance and adapt to market cycles.

Stay Informed and Educated

Stay informed about market trends, economic indicators, regulatory changes, and industry developments that may impact real estate market cycles and investment opportunities. Stay abreast of market research, industry reports, and expert analyses to gain insights into emerging trends, risks, and opportunities in the real estate market. Continuously educate yourself about evolving investment strategies, best practices, and innovative technologies to stay ahead of the curve and adapt to changing market conditions effectively.

Maintain a Long-Term Perspective

Maintain a long-term perspective in real estate investing and avoid reacting impulsively to short-term market fluctuations or noise. Focus on building a resilient and sustainable investment portfolio that can withstand market cycles and generate consistent returns over the long term. Resist the temptation to time the market or chase speculative trends, and instead focus on fundamental analysis, risk management, and value creation strategies that align with your long-term investment objectives and risk tolerance.

In conclusion, adapting to market cycles is essential for real estate investors to navigate the dynamic and cyclical nature of the real estate market effectively. By understanding market dynamics, diversifying portfolios, adopting flexible investment strategies, managing cash flow and liquidity, focusing on value-driven investments, monitoring portfolio allocation, staying informed and educated, and maintaining a long-term perspective, investors can capitalize on market opportunities, mitigate risks, and achieve success in the ever-changing real estate landscape.

Exit Strategies: Knowing When to Sell

Exit strategies are crucial for real estate investors to maximize returns, mitigate risks, and optimize portfolio performance. Knowing when to sell a property is just as important as knowing when to buy, as market conditions, investment objectives, and property dynamics may change over time. Effective exit strategies allow investors to capitalize on appreciation, unlock equity, rebalance portfolios, and reallocate capital to higher-yielding opportunities. In this chapter, we explore key considerations for determining when to sell a property and common exit strategies for real estate investors:

Market Conditions

Monitor market conditions and trends to assess the timing and feasibility of selling a property. Consider factors such as supply and demand dynamics, economic indicators, interest rates, demographic trends, and local market conditions. Sell properties during market upswings or peak periods when demand is high, competition is fierce, and property values are appreciating to maximize returns. Conversely, consider selling properties during market downturns or troughs to mitigate risks and preserve capital in anticipation of future market recovery.

Investment Objectives

Align your decision to sell with your investment objectives, risk tolerance, and financial goals. Evaluate whether the property continues to meet your investment criteria and contribute to your overall portfolio strategy. Determine whether selling the property aligns with your short-term liquidity needs, long-term growth objectives, tax planning strategies, or portfolio diversification goals. Assess the potential returns, risks, and opportunity costs associated with holding versus selling the property in light of your investment objectives and time horizon.

Property Performance

Assess the performance of the property relative to your investment expectations and benchmarks. Evaluate key performance metrics such as rental income, cash flow, occupancy rates, appreciation, and overall return on investment (ROI). Sell underperforming properties that fail to meet performance targets or generate satisfactory returns compared to alternative investment opportunities. Consider selling properties with declining cash flow, deteriorating market conditions, or significant capital expenditure requirements that may erode returns over time.

Equity Growth and Appreciation

Capitalize on equity growth and property appreciation to unlock value and realize profits from your investments. Sell properties when they have appreciated in value significantly or reached their full potential to capture capital gains and reinvest the proceeds into higher-yielding opportunities. Consider selling properties with substantial equity buildup or market appreciation to rebalance your portfolio, diversify investments, or fund future acquisitions, renovations, or strategic initiatives.

Tax Considerations

Evaluate the tax implications and consequences of selling a property to optimize tax efficiency and minimize tax liabilities. Consider factors such as capital gains taxes, depreciation recapture, tax-deferred exchanges, and passive activity loss limitations when planning your exit strategy. Consult with tax professionals or financial advisors to develop tax-efficient exit strategies, explore tax-deferral options, and maximize after-tax returns from property dispositions.

Market Demand and Buyer Profile

Assess market demand and buyer profile to determine the timing and approach for selling a property. Identify potential buyers, investors, or end-users who may be interested in acquiring the property based on their investment criteria, preferences, and financing capabilities. Tailor your marketing strategy, pricing strategy, and property presentation to appeal to target buyers and maximize market exposure. Leverage market demand, competitive bidding, and buyer competition to achieve favorable sale terms and maximize sale proceeds.

Exit Options and Strategies

Evaluate different exit options and strategies available for selling a property based on market conditions, investor preferences, and property characteristics. Consider traditional sales methods such as listing properties on the open market, engaging real estate agents, or conducting auctions. Explore alternative exit strategies such as seller financing, lease options, seller carryback financing, or 1031 exchanges to facilitate property sales, overcome market challenges, and optimize financial outcomes.

Risk Management and Portfolio Optimization

Use property sales as a strategic tool for risk management and portfolio optimization to align your investment portfolio with changing market conditions and investment objectives. Sell properties to reduce concentration risk, diversify asset allocation, or reallocate capital to higher-performing asset classes or market segments. Maintain a balanced portfolio mix that balances risk and return objectives while capitalizing on market opportunities and mitigating downside risks.

In conclusion, knowing when to sell a property is essential for real estate investors to maximize returns, mitigate risks, and optimize portfolio performance. By considering market conditions, investment objectives, property performance, equity growth, tax considerations, market demand, exit options, risk management, and portfolio optimization strategies, investors can develop effective exit strategies that align with their goals and achieve successful property dispositions in the dynamic and competitive real estate market.

Scaling Your Real Estate Portfolio

Scaling your real estate portfolio involves strategically expanding your property holdings, increasing asset value, and maximizing returns to achieve growth and diversification. Scaling requires careful planning, effective execution, and ongoing management to capitalize on investment opportunities, leverage resources, and mitigate risks. In this chapter, we explore key strategies for scaling your real estate portfolio:

Define Your Investment Goals

Clarify your investment goals, objectives, and risk tolerance to establish a clear roadmap for scaling your real estate portfolio. Determine your target portfolio size, asset allocation preferences, return targets, and timeline for growth. Align your investment strategy with your financial goals, whether it's generating passive income, building long-term wealth, achieving financial independence, or creating a legacy for future generations.

Develop a Scalable Investment Strategy

Develop a scalable investment strategy that enables you to expand your real estate portfolio systematically and sustainably over time. Consider factors such as market conditions, property types, geographic locations, investment criteria, financing options, and risk management strategies. Identify investment opportunities that align with your strategy and offer potential for value creation, capital appreciation, and income generation across different market cycles and economic environments.

Leverage Financing and Capital

Explore financing options and capital sources to fuel portfolio growth and leverage your investment capital more effectively. Consider traditional financing methods such as mortgages, bank loans, and commercial financing, as well as alternative sources such as private lenders, crowdfunding platforms, and syndication partnerships. Optimize your capital structure to minimize equity contributions, maximize leverage, and enhance return on investment while managing debt service obligations and liquidity risks responsibly.

Implement Systems and Processes

Implement systems, processes, and infrastructure to streamline portfolio management, operations, and decision-making as you scale your real estate holdings. Invest in technology tools, software platforms, and management systems to automate routine tasks, track performance metrics, and facilitate communication with tenants, vendors, and stakeholders. Develop standardized procedures for property acquisition, due diligence, leasing, property management, maintenance, and financial reporting to improve efficiency, consistency, and scalability.

Acquire Value-Add Opportunities

Seek value-add opportunities that offer potential for substantial returns and value creation through strategic renovations, repositioning, or redevelopment. Target properties with upside potential, distressed assets, or underperforming assets that can be acquired below market value and enhanced through value-added initiatives. Implement value-add strategies such as cosmetic upgrades, property improvements, operational optimizations, or rebranding efforts to increase property value, generate higher rental income, and accelerate portfolio growth.

Diversify Across Property Types and Markets

Diversify your real estate portfolio across different property types, asset classes, and geographic markets to spread risk, enhance resilience, and capitalize on diverse investment opportunities. Invest in a mix of residential, commercial, industrial, retail, and mixed-use properties to balance income stability, growth potential, and risk exposure. Allocate capital across multiple markets and regions to reduce concentration risk and leverage market-specific opportunities and trends.

Optimize Asset Management and Performance

Implement proactive asset management strategies to optimize portfolio performance, maximize returns, and enhance asset value as you scale your real estate portfolio. Monitor property performance, market trends, and tenant dynamics to identify opportunities for revenue enhancement, expense reduction, and operational efficiencies. Focus on maintaining high occupancy rates, maximizing rental income, controlling expenses, and preserving property value through proactive maintenance, tenant retention, and value-enhancing initiatives.

Evaluate Exit Strategies and Portfolio Optimization

Continuously evaluate exit strategies and portfolio optimization opportunities to rebalance your real estate portfolio, realize profits, and reinvest capital into higher-yielding opportunities. Assess market conditions, property performance, and investment objectives to determine the optimal timing and approach for property dispositions. Consider selling underperforming assets, recycling capital into higher-potential investments, or conducting 1031 exchanges to defer taxes and optimize portfolio composition.

In conclusion, scaling your real estate portfolio requires a strategic and disciplined approach that aligns with your investment goals, risk tolerance, and market opportunities. By defining your investment goals, developing a scalable strategy, leveraging financing and capital, implementing systems and processes, acquiring value-add opportunities, diversifying across property types and markets, optimizing asset management, and evaluating exit strategies, you can effectively scale your real estate portfolio and achieve long-term success in the dynamic and competitive real estate market.

Overcoming Common Pitfalls

Overcoming common pitfalls is essential for real estate investors to navigate the challenges and pitfalls that may arise during the investment process effectively. By identifying potential pitfalls and implementing proactive strategies to address them, investors can minimize risks, maximize returns, and achieve success in their real estate endeavors. In this chapter, we explore common pitfalls encountered by real estate investors and strategies for overcoming them:

Lack of Due Diligence

One of the most common pitfalls in real estate investing is inadequate due diligence, leading to unforeseen risks, liabilities, and financial losses. Overcome this pitfall by conducting thorough due diligence on properties, markets, and investment opportunities before making investment decisions.

Perform comprehensive property inspections, review financial records, assess market dynamics, and verify legal and regulatory compliance to mitigate risks and make informed investment choices.

Overleveraging

Overleveraging, or excessive use of debt, can increase financial risks and strain cash flow, especially during market downturns or economic downturns. Avoid overleveraging by maintaining a conservative debt-to-equity ratio, assessing your borrowing capacity, and structuring financing arrangements that align with your risk tolerance and investment objectives. Resist the temptation to overextend yourself or rely solely on debt financing to fund real estate acquisitions, and maintain adequate liquidity and reserves to weather market fluctuations and unforeseen expenses.

Underestimating Expenses

Underestimating expenses such as property maintenance, repairs, vacancies, and operating costs can erode cash flow and diminish investment returns over time. Overcome this pitfall by conducting thorough financial analysis and budgeting to accurately estimate expenses and cash flow projections. Factor in contingencies and reserve funds for unforeseen expenses, vacancies, or capital improvements to mitigate financial risks and ensure property profitability throughout the investment holding period.

Ignoring Market Trends

Ignoring market trends and failing to adapt to changing market conditions can lead to missed opportunities, poor investment decisions, and suboptimal returns. Stay informed about market trends, economic indicators, and industry developments to anticipate shifts in market dynamics and adjust your investment strategy accordingly. Monitor supply and demand dynamics, demographic trends, interest rates, and regulatory changes to identify emerging opportunities and risks in the real estate market and position yourself for success.

Overlooking Property Management

Neglecting property management responsibilities or partnering with inexperienced or unreliable property managers can result in tenant issues, operational inefficiencies, and property underperformance. Overcome this pitfall by prioritizing effective property management practices and selecting reputable, experienced property management partners. Establish clear communication channels, set performance expectations, and implement systems and procedures to ensure efficient property operations, tenant satisfaction, and asset performance.

Failing to Plan for Exit Strategies

Failing to plan for exit strategies or being unprepared for market downturns can limit flexibility and liquidity and impede portfolio optimization. Overcome this pitfall by developing comprehensive exit strategies for each investment property, considering various scenarios, market conditions, and investment objectives. Evaluate exit options such as property sales, refinancing, 1031 exchanges, or portfolio diversification to optimize returns, mitigate risks, and capitalize on market opportunities throughout the investment lifecycle.

Ignoring Legal and Regulatory Compliance

Ignoring legal and regulatory compliance requirements can expose investors to legal liabilities, fines, and litigation, jeopardizing investment success and reputation. Overcome this pitfall by prioritizing legal due diligence, adhering to applicable laws, regulations, and zoning ordinances, and seeking guidance from legal professionals when necessary. Stay informed about changes in local, state, and federal laws affecting real estate investments, such as landlord-tenant laws, fair housing regulations, environmental regulations, and tax laws, to ensure compliance and minimize legal risks.

Lack of Patience and Discipline

Impatience and lack of discipline can lead to impulsive investment decisions, chasing speculative trends, and abandoning long-term strategies prematurely. Overcome this pitfall by maintaining patience and discipline in your investment approach, sticking to your investment criteria, and avoiding emotional decision-making. Focus on fundamental analysis, risk management, and value-driven investment strategies that align with your long-term goals and risk tolerance, and resist the temptation to deviate from your investment plan based on short-term market fluctuations or external pressures.

In conclusion, overcoming common pitfalls in real estate investing requires diligence, discipline, and proactive risk management. By conducting thorough due diligence, avoiding overleveraging, accurately estimating expenses, staying informed about market trends, prioritizing effective property management, planning for exit strategies, complying with legal requirements, and maintaining patience and discipline, investors can navigate challenges effectively and achieve success in the dynamic and competitive real estate market.

The Future of Real Estate Investing

The future of real estate investing is evolving rapidly as technological advancements, demographic shifts, urbanization trends, and sustainability considerations reshape the landscape of the real estate market. Investors must anticipate and adapt to these changes to capitalize on emerging opportunities, mitigate risks, and achieve sustainable growth in their real estate portfolios. In this chapter, we explore key trends and insights shaping the future of real estate investing:

Technology Integration

Technology is revolutionizing every aspect of the real estate industry, from property search and transactions to construction methods and property management. Embrace technological innovations such as artificial intelligence (AI), big data analytics, virtual reality (VR), and blockchain technology to streamline operations, enhance decision-making, and optimize asset performance. Leverage PropTech solutions for property valuation, market analysis, tenant engagement, smart building management, and digital transactions to gain a competitive edge and maximize returns.

Evolving Consumer Preferences

Changing demographics, lifestyles, and preferences are driving demand for innovative real estate solutions that cater to diverse needs and preferences. Adapt to shifting consumer preferences by investing in flexible, multifunctional spaces, mixed-use developments, co-living arrangements, and experiential amenities that appeal to modern tenants and occupiers. Embrace sustainability, wellness, and community-centric design principles to create environments that foster well-being, productivity, and social connectivity, resonating with the preferences of millennial and Gen Z renters and buyers.

Rise of Urbanization and Mixed-Use Developments

Urbanization trends are fueling demand for mixed-use developments that offer a blend of residential, commercial, retail, and entertainment amenities in walkable, transit-oriented neighborhoods. Capitalize on urbanization trends by investing in urban infill projects, transit-oriented developments, and mixed-use communities that cater to the growing demand for live-work-play environments. Create vibrant, mixed-use destinations that integrate residential, retail, office, and recreational spaces to enhance livability, convenience, and connectivity for residents and tenants.

Focus on Sustainability and ESG Investing

Environmental, social, and governance (ESG) considerations are increasingly influencing real estate investment decisions as investors prioritize sustainability, resilience, and responsible investing practices. Integrate sustainability initiatives, green building certifications, energy-efficient design features, and renewable energy solutions into real estate projects to reduce environmental impact, enhance asset value, and attract environmentally conscious tenants and investors. Embrace ESG investing principles to align with investor preferences, mitigate risks, and create long-term value for stakeholders.

Alternative Asset Classes and Investment Vehicles

Real estate investors are diversifying their portfolios and exploring alternative asset classes and investment vehicles beyond traditional property types. Consider investing in niche sectors such as healthcare, life sciences, data centers, logistics, and affordable housing to capitalize on specialized market segments and emerging trends.

Explore alternative investment vehicles such as real estate investment trusts (REITs), real estate crowdfunding platforms, and private equity funds to access diversified portfolios, passive income streams, and attractive risk-adjusted returns in the real estate market.

Globalization and Cross-Border Investments

Globalization trends and cross-border capital flows are driving international real estate investment activity as investors seek opportunities beyond domestic markets. Explore global real estate markets, emerging economies, and cross-border investment opportunities to diversify geographic exposure, access growth markets, and leverage currency arbitrage. Partner with local experts, developers, and operators to navigate regulatory, cultural, and market complexities in international markets and capitalize on global real estate investment trends.

Adaptation to Demographic Shifts

Demographic shifts, including aging populations, urbanization, and workforce mobility, are reshaping demand patterns and investment preferences in the real estate market. Adapt to demographic trends by investing in senior housing, active adult communities, urban apartments, and transit-oriented developments that cater to evolving lifestyle preferences and demographic needs. Consider the impact of demographic changes on housing demand, retail preferences, office space requirements, and healthcare services to align investments with demographic shifts and long-term demand trends.

Resilience and Risk Management

Climate change, natural disasters, and geopolitical uncertainties pose risks to real estate investments, emphasizing the importance of resilience and risk management strategies. Incorporate resilience measures, disaster preparedness, and climate risk assessments into real estate investment decision-making to mitigate physical, financial, and regulatory risks associated with climate-related hazards. Invest in resilient infrastructure, sustainable design features, and adaptive strategies that enhance property resilience, minimize risk exposure, and safeguard long-term investment value in the face of environmental and geopolitical challenges.

In conclusion, the future of real estate investing is characterized by technological innovation, evolving consumer preferences, urbanization trends, sustainability considerations, alternative asset classes, globalization, demographic shifts, and resilience imperatives. By embracing these trends, adapting to market dynamics, and leveraging emerging opportunities, real estate investors can navigate the evolving landscape of the real estate market successfully and achieve sustainable growth and value creation in their investment portfolios.

www.ingramcontent.com/pod-product-compliance
Lightning Source LLC
Chambersburg PA
CBHW050315230526
45471CB00005B/2188